Sleeping and Waking

SLEEPING AND WAKING

Michael O'Brien

Flood Editions

Chicago

For permission, required to reprint or
broadcast more than several lines, write to:
Flood Editions, Post Office Box 3865
Chicago, Illinois 60654-0865
www.floodeditions.com

ISBN 0-9787467-2-4

Cover illustration: Joan Farber, *Slievemore,
Curling Fog* (2002), courtesy of the artist.
Design and composition by Quemadura

Printed on acid-free, recycled paper
in the United States of America

This book was made possible in part
through a grant from the Illinois Arts Council

The author wishes to thank the Tanne Foundation
for an award in 2002; the Achill Heinrich
Böll Committee for a residency in the
Böll cottage, Achill Island, Co. Mayo, Ireland;
The Elephantine Press, publisher of *Six Poems* (2003),
and Pressed Wafer, publisher of a foldup (2005),
where some of these poems first appeared;
Westbeth for a reading; Hiroaki Sato for the sense of
two Japanese poems; and Allen Brafman for a push.

for Joan

CONTENTS

Sleeping and Waking

CERTAIN EVENINGS

To some the world is given in images, to some in sentences. To some it's given as a smack in the head from an unseen hand, but that is not this story. If it is a story. Things happen in stories: a kind of intravenous drip of happenings. That is not this story. This is the story of a man sitting in a room writing everything down that comes into his head. Images and sentences. A kind of parade. That ends at the cemetery. Laying wreaths on the graves. As the volleys are fired, three of them, and their echoes. The commands surprising in the spring air, as much a part of the rifles as their bolts. All the little flags. That fade as the year advances. Members of the band leaning on their elbows in the grass, among their instruments. And then changing it. What he's written down. The man in the room. So that what happens is the changes. This is the story.

■

In Penn Station an archaic music so serene it cannot be happening fills the great rotunda with snow. Something drags on the escalator, some impediment, the metal howls as each step lifts to its level and disappears. Two sentences proceed in parallel, indifferent, wearing away the listener's attention. The travelers and their purposes have come to rest, waiting for the great trains. On the concourse new arrivals drift in numbers past the watchers, immobilized, practicing stillness, each attending the announcement of the one event, forsaking all others.

■

An advertisement the size of a six-story building, plastered onto its wall: the huge photo, the girl, the clothes, the model's puzzled, blank defiance, life translated into some other language, one it cannot support. In the upper-left-hand corner, out of scale, the eye snags on, cannot make sense of, what prove to be two windows, actual windows, plants in them, people behind them getting on with their lives. Or not. With this ad pasted over them, which of course they can't see, leaning on the windowsill, six floors up, looking out at the traffic on Houston.

■

Radio voices from the apartment below, human cadences, their meanings washed away, a muttering of doves. Music heard in the subway, from another platform, before the train obliterates everything: your first recognition is that it's music, not what music. Speech itself, free of designation. As if the walls spoke. Two schoolgirls in uniform by the Cheyenne Diner, sharing a cigarette before class.

■

A bank and a supermarket stand next to each other on one of the avenues near New York Hospital. Each has a sidewalk facility, one dispensing money, one receiving bottles and returning the deposits on them. Some days two columns form, those with bank accounts, those with great sacks of empties, shuffling forward together. In silence. To the tip. Like traffic, magnificent, the sun comes and goes.

■

A small, pot-bellied woman in a bright green dress speaks antiphonal, incomprehensible sentences by the Seventh Avenue subway, possessed, testifying, warning, rocking in place with the voices, their repeating decimal, ghosts that feed on speech. Nearby a man, head raised, eyes closed, is drinking the sunlight. He takes his time. His thirst is great.

■

Black fades to grey in the clothes of the homeless. A beaky, ageless woman with quick, guarded eyes, all her stuff divided between two shopping carts and some plastic bags, moves down Ninth Avenue. She leaves one cart, goes a few steps with the other; stops; leaves the other, returns to the first, brings it up to the other; stops; sets out again. Like a defective purgatory no one remembers the point of, or how to turn it off. Like being hazed by one's needs. By human practice. Which can change.

GHOSTS

Fake Greek temple
corner of Eighth &
14th used to be a
bank now sells carpets

■

Highway
     sign
Wrapped in
     burlap
It means
     Nothing

■

Please
stand clear of the
clos-
ing do's

FOR CAMERON BROWN

It comes round, weather,
feelings, in clouds, in
strata, the shapes of
the day, pegged to their
shadows, shift, marry,
on their way, gone to the
changes, those heavy
dates that we keep.

UPSTATE

First raindrops, a
cat's footprints, the
wiper
opens its fan.

■

In a broken
dream I have
just met Lord
Byron, '30s suit,
cocktail lounge, Graham
Greene's opaque, intelligent
face, eyes that have
seen everything, a
spider's eyes, a
kind of banked
fury. What is
dark mops up
the light. I
reach for my
watch to see

where we are
in night's program.

.

In the night
bear climbs onto
the porch, a
clumsy sound, later
I hear him
come back but
it was thunder.

.

Stirred by the
least wind the
wintry, carrot-
colored willow.

.

A pickup
full of snow,
a crow's rau-
cous laugh, the
rapids comb-
ing its hair.

AFTER LU YU

Road dust & winestains
on my clothes, a

long journey, everywhere
reminded of things.

What does it take to
be a poet? In the drizzle I

ride my donkey
through the Saber Gate.

UNDER SLIEVEMORE

Past all hovering the
runnel clears the last
stones of its channel, loosed
into air itself, spray
parting in wind. *Follow me down.*

■

Huge underwater
shadows race outward, the
tide comes
filling the bay.

■

Thin skin of
life, sundown's
darting bird, ocean
sliding over rock, a
wound closing.

■

Cloud touches
mountain so lightly,

folded into the folds,
on its slow way.

■

Flicker of two white
moths in grass
interferes with
day's pattern, monolith.

■

On wiry stems the
tufts of bog cotton
bob in wind.
Rainclouds darken Slievemore.

■

Patches of lighter, darker
green fade to darker
green, grey stone, to
mottled grey at the
top, cloudless a moment,
neither heavy nor light,
without attribute.

■

The pulse of it:
sideways, in veils, in
windy columns a fine,
penetrant rain
crosses the hillside.

■

All night the wind
hammers at whatever
stands in its way. Insists. Will not
take no for an answer.

■

Great, startled heron
struggles up from the bog,
pistons the air,
gone over hillside.

■

Likeness washes
across things without a
trace, a cloud's
shadow in a field.

■

Wind thrashing &
banging in the
trees, a populous
sound, seething in
thickets, wet dark
at the end of
the long summer day.

■

Birds' voices
hang in mid-air.
Red cow & her calf
browse in the dale.
Bogdark water
runs by the road.
Sunlight clusters
on Blacksod Bay.

AFTER KIYOHARA MOTOSUKE

I wish I could bring
home the brocade of
that autumn field of
bush clover, deer
snorting in the brushwood.

CONFETTI

vernacular
rain

Jeez
Sheesh

Multiscam
Pisces Meatball

sleepers
loosies

Melon Cola
Techni Cola

Da Costa Demolition

precip
coma toes

A PILLOW BOOK, CONTINUED

—You're the least stoical person I've ever known.

—All I want is someone to tell me it's all right.

—The stoic tells *himself* it's all right.

Little wake in the elevator.

A yawn of pure anxiety, unadulterated by boredom or fatigue.

Seated girl carefully eating a pear on the Seventh Avenue local.

—You think the world is coming to get you. I think the world is the boat I've missed.

Little sleeps.

—My father would have liked this.

—You must like it for him.

Two men stand talking on the corner of 24th, waiting for the light to change so one can cross Ninth Avenue to the newsstand and buy a lottery ticket. As he starts out his friend says *Don't pick nothin' strange.*

The world as airport. The book of days.

The doorman draws on his magician gloves.

"You make a world, you fix it with shims."

Consciousness & delay.

Pshaw! says the huge truck, braking.

Sometimes the words themselves know. *The Catholic Cate-chism* by Father Hardon. *The World of Damages.*

Sudden crazy song & dance of the man on 23rd, TV routines burned into his brain decades ago.

The blur of *whatever*. Hands thrown up, the hopelessness of words.

Lace-curtain English.

The wheelchair of the man with cerebral palsy has tipped over backwards with him in it just by the door of the waiting school-bus, and though he is picked up and set right again, he howls, gathers breath, howls again—for he cannot speak—in rage and terror.

—Why stir up old stuff?
—There is no old stuff.

Vexations. The paranoid apathy induced by an evening of television. The flypaper of Christmas. Suety voices shilling classical music. People who are right and insufferable. Losing a glove.

Piling up a progression of chords that helplessly bring about the resolution they are trying to stave off.

Synecdoche. Wash your face and hope for the best.

A Dictionary of the History of Ideas, illus.

Not to live a newspaper life.

The pom-poms of the car exhausts.

Dawn, horizon, fracture of light.

ONCE

on the street she
yawns, her jeans
yawn, her knees
rhyme with her eyes

■

helpless, half-suppressed
smile of the
girl in the
Bleecker Street subway,
trying hard not to
beam across at her sweetie

■

work against correspondence, the
world is not a
book, everything is
not something else, you
could look it up

INSIDE

old barn, earth
floor, a
darkness, some
chips of light

.

dark butterfly of the
lungs, opening
&
closing its wings

HEADACHE

pats at the walls
of the skull. If
it touches a switch
there you will throw
up. Lie still. Try
to let nothing slip.

FEVER

Hot in here.
Joints ache, slow
breath changes
gear. Edging
toward sleep a
dry clarity of
vision tips
into hallucination.
Someone has
gone through the
house turning
lights on &
off. Someone
has picked me
up & dropped me.

FROM AN OLD NOTEBOOK

Day is out of
breath, cadenza
without issue, the
nightmare pulp

huge building
shadows the park, who
dream of being
inside the cock

an eddy of
ghosts, an
old plastic bag
turning in circles

negatives of a
monument, a
valise, a
dream sponsored by the state.

THE MARK

Last year's palms
burnt to ash.
    Every spring he is
tortured to death
for my priceless
worthless sins.
Sponsored by his
father. Would I
care to watch?
    This
porno flick, this
lust to burn
the world away.
    A priest's
smudged thumbprint
on each pale forehead.

ANOTHER AUTUMN

slenderest of new moons, surfer's sail transparent as an
   insect's wing

day drowses, breathless, leaf, then butterfly, each with the
   same spot of rust

word of worst omen, *metastasized*, saturating the media

an old starving actor, a defrocked priest with an evil
   conscience

a television set left on in the room, a furniture-music

little cloud of marijuana on Hudson Street where someone
   lit up

the brick of meaning, the brick of money, you want to muss
   up their hair

if he says *Do not hasten to bid me adieu* he's not a cowboy

a feathering of the ink whereby characters lose definition

overlapping windowscreens, one pattern interfering with
   another

sideways, all that politeness, all that irony, trying for a draw

dead language of our conversations, what will life put up in
   your place

a day gradually effacing itself, perfecting its absence

larval suns, asleep, the handspan of nothing between ribs
   & pelvis

flaking newsprint, rust's slow fire, a photo yellowing like
   seersucker

stipple of rain on pond, talking to itself, the day's vacant places

coins of the leaves spangle the lawn, a jet tears off a piece of
   the sky

four gulls rise, fall, at the lip of the wave, a kindergarten music

night train, broken sighs, sleepers' pillows wag like Mother
   Superior

tiny rainbow of spilt gas in asphalt puddle, its hospital tuck

something busted and homemade, a father, a margin, away·
    from them

rain beads on fire escape, neon spring, we watched every
    chorus come home

IN MAINE

I

Tree-wraiths in
fog, wind-clatter, a

rash of
lichen-flowers.

Many clouds marry
the one mountain.

■

Suddenly everywhere
tiny moths
like leaves falling.

■

Down by the
marsh little
fans of the
spiderwebs,
cones, transmitters,

all turned a-
way from the
rising sun.

∎

Lying in bed
figuring out what you're hearing

long conversation of the rain

slow comfortable sound
wind volleying across

& the rain bears down
like someone who won't take no for an answer.

2

Backroad cemetery, stones
in their ranks, their good
order, desks in
elementary school, all
the carved names

■

Learned, then lost, word
gone out like a
light   *viburnum*

terror of the hawk's shadow

3

Hanks of red
seaweed trail from
the branches of
a half-fallen
tree along the
shingle, stones still
tight in its roots.

Clouds mass over
water, sky closed,
sealed off, one gap,
a long, fluted
column of light
strikes at the bay's
hurried waters.

SALAMANDERS

days like
architecture, days whose
columns
hold up the sky

■

loaves in their
crocks, slowly
rising in the
baker's window

■

pounding like breath, wave
upon wave, in the
gap a gull's shadow
crosses the water

■

walls of
light, wells
of light

FOR DICK & TERESA

At the
threshold of

sound, wind
chimes. Under

tangled apple
boughs four

chairs dumbshow
a conversation.

AFTER ÔTAKA GENGO TADASUKE

Surely there will be a
teahouse where we can
drink among plum blossoms
on our way to the other world.

UKULELE SONGS

Moonlight: is
this
thick or
thin?

■

Tiny
horns of the
speedwell.

■

Two crows
or one
crow &
its shadow.

■

These are the
bones you
have to move.

∎

So who is
breathing whom?

THOSE DAYS

She was heading for the
canto, he was heading for
the fragment, she was trying
to put something together, a
center, work there, he was
trying to take something
apart, find the exit, go.

■

like a cool drink
like I was music she was reading

■

sparrow in the dumpsters
no one's bird, tougher
than Catullus who no
longer belongs to himself

EPHEMERA

driving into the
sunset, the bright
cars, the vapor
trails' bright scars

∎

in low grass the
spiders' pavilions

∎

plastered to the
wall a tiny
moth, batwings
intricate as footnotes

FOURTH OF JULY

trees sway, wind
lifts their branches like a sea

the river disappears in brightness

the rocket, tadpole, spirals up

HUSH

black cat darting
into roadside grass,
a passing
car's shadow

.

tiny spider in the
teaspoon, no, the
huge chandelier
reflected there

WHAT SHE DOES

She takes his weight as
bare trees take January
light, as
mind remembers the
secret consonants of
French words, as the
student comes to the
hard place in Virgil
with an intake of
breath, as the sleeper
breaks up in the
dream descending the
stair, as gravity,
appetite, rain draw us
down, homemade,
ad lib, as the
willow takes the
wind, leaves flashing
silver as it turns

SLEEPING AND WAKING

Breeze ripples the
buildings' long veils

Projector, tireless
in the empty room

■

They hide in
the crowd, call
Number to
rescue them

■

On and on, steady as the
locusts in
summer's furnace, the
nerves' high, wordless song

■

The person waking is
not the one in the
familiar unraveling

dream the one with
another life who now
on the stair forgets
you as you forget him

■

He closes his eyes
with appetite

eyes grasping at darkness

■

Little grimace, flicker
of distaste, moment
someone's resolve is
set on death. Dull
wintry body from which
love has withdrawn.

■

Holding one end of the
dream. Incomprehensible.
A bird trying to
tell you how it flies

■

paresthesia, slow
burn, the
nerves playing
bait & switch
something
happening, just not here

■

hugging sleep to
himself like lost
love, sleeper in
his pod of warmth

■

Taking the opiate he
lies in the dark watching
pain recede to a
pinpoint of light. *Bravo!*
he wants to say but
the drug drives on and
now he sleeps

■

walks out
into the
light that has
come so far

wipers sifting the
day, shoals of
light on the river, the
willow's shower of gold

.

ribbon of
flame

pinned to its
hunger

THE SLEEPER

enters the city
mirage of his death

observes the willow
unpack its leaves

proves noon's stadium
headline roar

through his mind
passes a river

a diagrammed sentence
unfailing

clouds like nerves
day a quarry of light

THE VISITATION

Napkins! forgotten
in the fuss of
breakfast. *Napkins*
would be nice! Sprang

up, anxious to
put things right, heard
Howard say, once,
firmly, *Napkins.* As

if to say, *This*
is not worth haste.
Not worth confusion.
Calm down. Speak di-

rectly. Say what
matters. Many words
to gloss his one. He
was on my side.

FRACTURE

X-ray parts hand's
cloud of flesh:
two bright screws join
broken bone.

Behind my shield, my
plaster shell, I
study
to make a fist.

GLOSS ON STEVENS

The impatient
spirit's appetites,
for which the world
is finger-food.

osprey, via
Old French from
Latin *ossifraga*,
"the bonebreaker"

LOCAL

Opens her *Times* like a
logical argument
shaking the pages as
if to be rid of the
worst of the news.

■

You live with the grid, it
tells you where you are, you
get used to it. Then one
day it starts to feel like
a graph with your present
position & all its
projections plotted out.
Last Wash 7 pm.

■

He had lost
something in sleep, was
determined to
look for it there,

could see that the
world was on fire, coals
burning just under
the transparent crust.

.

Passing the window his
body looks like a
shed built onto . . .
onto what. His head. Air.

Now: with this equipment
Straighten up and
fly right. That's what the
old song says. Yowsah.

.

kicks off with the
left going down, a
bell lifting
off from its clapper

now breath turns to speech
now the obliterating trains

.

jewelry, stigmata,
dress a wrapper to
tear off, commodity
approaching its limit

∎

At a
party my
father suddenly
appears, young,
vigorous, I'm
so glad to
see him it
wakes me up.

∎

The cardboard box
on 20th St.
that an appliance
came in is
now someone's house.

∎

sleep
dark water

a flock
of birds turning

a deck
of cards dealt out

all fade
like frost on grass

■

In all the street eye
catches on the one
spot of light, a
cellphone's blue TV glare.

BRIEFINGS

"People are
fungible. You

can have them
here or there.

You understand
it. Everyone

in the room
understands it."

∎

The horror
movies were

training films,
proposed a

world without
limits where

what might be
done might be

accepted. We
were practicing.

■

Aeneas stares
down at Avernus

black jaws so foul the
Greeks called the place

Aornon: Birdless.

The Sibyl tells him
this is the easy part.

WALKING THE DOG

"To be men not destroyers." And the Cantos stop.
"DESTROYERS" written in wet concrete on 22nd St.
as if a vote had been cast. A sign for
"HISTORIES" resolves to "IN STORES."
With each breath of wind more petals sift down.

GOING TO SLEEP

"For as

long as

the song lasts."

∎

Shall.

To.

"What a country!"

∎

He meets a woman in a fairgrounds, statuesque, calm, unsurprised. She wears a white knit dress, close-fitting round her breasts, which are large and prominent, and a large-brimmed hat on the back of her head. She's beautiful, a goddess out of a '30s movie. Her whole body is like an erection, and he has one. He embraces her with ardor, she's distracted, turns away, says *Why do you call so often?* He's thinking, *Where do we go?* as people do when they urgently need a place to go and there is none.

SOME OF THE NAMES

All Sunday long in
slow rain rags of
clouds trace the
gullies of Mt. Shaw.

■

glasses, enters
them, the
horse, the
harness

■

If there were
Furies they might
sound like the
baffled currents roaming
these elevator shafts

■

jewelweed's orange
scalloped horn
hangs by a thread and
summer drives on

■

dog-day locust
flail of its cry

AS IT HAPPENS

brushy, the
sound of traffic: you
figure it's raining,
go back to sleep,

start over: birds
winch up the day,
the highway's stoplights
hooded like falcons

three horses and
their shadows, long
dark patches on
the early grass

flattened by
love, its
color exhausted, a
rain-spent morning glory

passing radio, rosary
drone of a rapper,
bike messengers
flickering like glowworms

Purity of heart is
to will one thing, the
acres of
exquisite rubble

cauldron of
morning: they are
setting up in the
parking lots,

old things turned
over and over: smoke
cut off by
wind at chimney lip,

hurried away:
as if the light
were interrupting
darkness: *what*

cannot be mended,
the days
wearing themselves
out, the

broken letters
to be discarded, a
bird's footprint
melting in snow.

SOME OF THE DAYS

so much sleep
poured into a
vessel it can
hold no more

■

days without traction, their
dream-jukebox, over the
bones of sleep where in flood
the river rewrites itself

■

calm lake whereon
boat of the breath

AFTER HIPPOCRATES

Life is short, art long, the moment swift, one stumbles trying,
    choice is hard.
And all the while the body is talking to itself, susurrus of
information, incessant, unnoticed. Gusts of light cross a facade,
traceless print of the day, it has come so far, this movie, tireless,
even when the room is empty. Or thunder comes, preoccupied,
moving heavy furniture, muttering, pronouncing the broken
hundred-syllabled name of a god. You stop on the sidewalk
    and the
river of people divides around you, flows on, and you
move and are one with it: sparrows quick as dice on the fire
    escape,
facades, the tremendous sky, sunset after sunset as the bus
moves down Ninth Avenue. A huge crane places a dot at the
    end of a sentence,
pigeons wheel, now black, now white, we paste the days
    together with sleep,
draft horses huge as horses in dreams. Dawn has in reserve
    so much light,
seeping into the streets, saturating them, turning up in a place
    where no eye but would see.

Michael O'Brien was born in Granville, New York in 1939; studied at Fordham, the University of Paris, and Columbia; worked as a librarian; was one of the Eventorium poets, where his first book was published in 1967; taught at Brooklyn and Hunter; worked for many years editing technical publications; wrote *The Summer Poems, Conversations at the West End, Blue Springs, Veil, Hard Rain, The Ruin, The Floor and the Breath, 17 Songs, At Schoodic, Sills, Six Poems, Swift Moons Repair Celestial Losses*, and *Sleeping and Waking*. He lives in New York City.